Luke

# DISCOVER TOGETHER BIBLE STUDY SERIES

*Leader's guides are available at www.discovertogetherseries.com*

# Luke

*Discovering Healing in
Jesus' Words to Women*

## Sue Edwards

 Kregel Publications

*Luke: Discovering Healing in Jesus' Words to Women*
© 2012 by Sue Edwards

Published by Kregel Publications, a division of Kregel, Inc., P.O. Box 2607, Grand Rapids, MI 49501.

Previously published by Kregel Publications as *Luke: Finding Truth and Healing in Jesus' Words to Women*, © 2009 by Sue Edwards.

All Scripture quotations are taken from the Holy Bible, New International Version®, NIV®. Copyright © 1973, 1978, 1984, 2011 by Biblica, Inc.™ Used by permission of Zondervan. All rights reserved worldwide. www.zondervan.com

ISBN 978-0-8254-4310-7

Printed in the United States of America

16 / 5 4 3 2

# Contents

*— Sally, De. 4*

# How to Get the Most Out of a Discover Together Bible Study

**W**omen today need Bible study to keep balanced, focused, and Christ-centered in their busy worlds. The tiered questions in *Luke: Discovering Healing in Jesus' Words to Women* allow you to choose a depth of study that fits your lifestyle, which may even vary from week to week, depending on your schedule.

Just completing the basic questions will require about one and a half hours per lesson, and will provide a basic overview of the text. For busy women, this level offers in-depth Bible study with a minimum time commitment.

"Digging Deeper" questions are for those who want to, and make time to, probe the text even more deeply. Answering these questions may require outside resources such as an atlas, Bible dictionary, or concordance; you may be asked to look up parallel passages for additional insight; or you may be encouraged to investigate the passage using an interlinear Greek-English text or *Vine's Expository Dictionary*. This deeper study will challenge you to learn more about the history, culture, and geography related to the Bible, and to grapple with complex theological issues and differing views. Some with teaching gifts and an interest in advanced academics will enjoy exploring the depths of a passage, and might even find themselves creating outlines and charts and writing essays worthy of seminarians!

This inductive Bible study is designed for both individual and group discovery. You will benefit most if you tackle each week's lesson on your own, and then meet with other women to share insights, struggles, and aha moments. Bible study leaders will find free, downloadable leader's guides for each study, along with general tips for leading small groups, at www.discovertogetherseries.com.

Through short video clips, Sue Edwards shares personal insights to enrich your Bible study experience. You can watch these as you work through each lesson on your own, or your Bible study leader may want your whole study group to view them when you meet together. For ease of individual

viewing, a QR code, which you can simply scan with your smartphone, is provided in each lesson. Or you can go to www.discovertogetherseries.com and easily navigate until you find the corresponding video title. Woman-to-woman, these clips are meant to bless, encourage, and challenge you in your daily walk.

Choose a realistic level of Bible study that fits your schedule. You may want to finish the basic questions first, and then "dig deeper" as time permits. Take time to savor the questions, and don't rush through the application. Watch the videos. Read the sidebars for additional insight to enrich the experience. Note the optional passage to memorize and determine if this discipline would be helpful for you. Do not allow yourself to be intimidated by women who have more time or who are gifted differently.

Make your Bible study—whatever level you choose—top priority. Consider spacing your study throughout the week so that you can take time to ponder and meditate on what the Holy Spirit is teaching you. Do not make other appointments during the group Bible study. Ask God to enable you to attend faithfully. Come with an excitement to learn from others and a desire to share yourself and your journey. Give it your best, and God promises to join you on this adventure that can change your life.

# Why Study Luke?

What if Jesus invited you to lunch? What would you talk about? What concerns would you divulge? How might the interaction affect you? Dozens of first-century women experienced a face-to-face encounter with Jesus, and, in a sense, we can too, as we "eavesdrop." Luke recorded many of these conversations in his gospel.

Each of the four gospels was written to a different audience for a different purpose. Luke's gospel is the gospel to the Gentiles, to the little people, and to women, who were undervalued in the first century. C. S. Lewis wrote, ". . . for the little, low, timid, warped, thin-blooded, lonely people—or the passionate, sensual, unbalanced people—if they make any attempt at goodness at all, they learn, in double-quick time, that they need help. It is Christ or nothing for them. It is taking up the cross and following—or else despair. They are the lost sheep; He came especially to find them" (*Mere Christianity*, 181). I so relate.

There are forty-three references to women in Luke's gospel. Obviously, Jesus cared for first-century women, and he cares for you. Let's explore these conversations together, and don't expect to walk away the same as when you arrived. Nancy Ortberg wrote, "Jesus' interactions with people rarely left them unchanged. He stirred things up and shook people's wrong ideas of God. He made heroes out of the most unlikely people and challenged thinking and lifestyles. He didn't end conversations by saying 'You're great just the way you are; don't ever change. Let's do lunch.'"

 **Introduction to Studying Luke** (*5:10 minutes*).

# Replace Control with Trust

## *Mary, the Mother of Jesus*

It's easier to relinquish control and trust God when we are children, before life's trials and heartaches open up a realm of sobering possibilities we never knew existed.

from "Mary's Prayer"

And tiny feet cupped in the palm of my hand, rest. For many difficult steps lie ahead for you.

Do you taste the dust of the trails you will travel?

Do you feel the cold sea water upon which you will walk?

Do you wrench at the invasion of the nail you will bear? . . .

Rest, tiny feet. Rest today so that tomorrow you might walk with power. Rest. For millions will follow in your steps.

—Max Lucado, *God Came Near*

(p. 18; reprinted by permission)

Mary, the mother of Jesus, experienced an amazing life of adventure, ecstasy, and tragedy. Like most mothers, she wanted the best for her son—the Son—and sometimes struggled to entrust him into God the Father's care. Put yourself in her shoes as we journey through her life as revealed in the gospel accounts. What can you learn from Mary to enrich and strengthen your own walk with the Savior?

 Read Luke 1:26–38.

## THE ADVENTURE BEGINS

1. Jewish girls were betrothed in their early teens, which leads many scholars to believe Mary could have been thirteen or fourteen when the angel Gabriel announced that she would be the mother of the

Being born a human was not the first time God made Himself small so that we could have access to Him. First He shrunk Himself when He revealed the Torah at Mount Sinai. He shrunk Himself into tiny Hebrew words, man's finite language, so that we might get to Him that way. Then He shrunk Himself again, down to the size of a baby, down into manger finiteness.

—Lauren Winner
(*Girl Meets God*, 74)

Biblical women spent two-thirds or more of their lives giving birth and mothering in contrast to women today who, on average, spend only about one-seventh of their lives birthing and caring for children.

—Miriam Feinberg Vamosh
(*Women*, 42)

long awaited Messiah. Describe the conversation between Mary and Gabriel in Luke 1:34–38. What surprises you about her response?

*That she was so willing to comply!*

2. Mary experienced an unplanned pregnancy. How do you think her family, friends, and neighbors would have reacted if they knew?

*Probably disagreed, esp. when Joseph denied being the father.*

3. Have you ever been misunderstood, yet unable to explain yourself? What happened? How did you feel? What do you think would have been your response if you had found yourself in Mary's shoes?

*Yes, when Benny died — was horrible. Don't know. Hope I would have been aware that an angel was speaking to me! But, then how would I have explained that?*

 Read Luke 1:39–45.

## THE GIFT OF A MENTOR

4. Mary immediately set out for the home of Elizabeth, a trusted relative who was also miraculously pregnant. How did Elizabeth react when Mary unexpectedly came through the door (1:42–45)?

*She immediately recognized what had happened to Mary when her unborn child leaped of joy – and she welcomed her and congratulated her on her obedience to God.*

5. What impact do you think Elizabeth's words had on Mary? How would you have felt?

*I would have felt confirmed in what I had agreed to do – and relieved to have an advocate!*

6. Has God ever provided you with a trusted friend or mentor at just the right time? If so, please share.

*Yes – Sherry!*

 **Read Luke 1:46–55 aloud.**

## A JUBILANT SONG

7. Mary responds to these events with a beautiful outburst of worship. What themes run through her song? What words does she use to describe God? What can you learn about this young girl from these verses?

   _She is grateful for God's trust in her, feels honored — and then praises Hin for loving the lowly, keeping his covenant w/ abraham_

8. Some of us came to faith as children, others in youth or as adults. If you came to faith in Jesus as a child, describe ways your faith affected your early years. What are the advantages of trusting Christ as a child? As an adult?

   _As a child I learned the OT and NT stories, learned to pray, sang wonderful hymns. Church became another home for me, a place where I first loved and deposited_

9. Consider Mary's responses to Gabriel's announcement. What kind of faith and trust does she display? We know nothing about her childhood. Nevertheless, what would you surmise about her childhood relationship with Almighty God?

*At first she's perplexed, but then seems to understand that she's to birth the Messiah that has been long predicted. She knows scripture and God's line of the righteous.*

 Read Luke 2:1–20.

## AN UNUSUAL BIRTH

10. How do you think Mary was feeling about traveling during the final days of her pregnancy and then delivering her baby in a strange, unknown place (2:5–7)? If you are a mother, what was your emotional and physical state just before your child was born? What would have been your natural reaction if you had been Mary?

*I would have been anxious — and afraid — no shelter, noone to help w/ the birth other than Joseph. She must have wondered how a child of God would end up in such a place as a lowly manger.*

God among us! What a miracle! It had been planned for all eternity. It was for your redemption and for mine. The ramifications of that birth are enormous and are by no means all worked out yet. "God was in Christ, reconciling the world unto Himself."
—Ray Ortland
(*Intersections*, 17)

11. What was Mary's response to this amazing and challenging birth (2:19)?

*She cherished it — and pondered it.*

12. Recall a time when you "treasured" an experience and "pondered it in your heart" (perhaps, for example, a ministry opportunity, a friendship, a new job, a relationship). How did the experience change you? Did it increase your trust in God? If so, how?

*My _____ in ___ and very rooming up ____ Moore.*

*Prayer gp. in Parkersburg ...*

13. Mary probably had not expected to give birth to Jesus in a town far away from home under these conditions. Can you remember a time when circumstances did not work out as you had hoped? Did you make the best of the situation or did you fight with God? Did you try to control or manipulate the events to your liking? How can we prepare now to trust God in the midst of life's difficulties?

- Raising Uba.
- HF / Viet Nam - 7 yrs. instead of 5 !

In first-century Israel, women usually helped other women during the birthing process, which makes me wonder if women of Bethlehem helped Mary when she was in labor with Jesus, even though she was a stranger. The strong tradition of hospitality favors the possibility.  —Sue

14. Read Micah 5:2, the words of an Old Testament prophet spoken centuries earlier. What can you learn about God from this prophecy and the events in Luke 2:1–6?

Micah predicts that Jesus would be born in Bethlehem —
Our time is not necessarily God's timing — but God can be trusted.

Was Mary married to Joseph before they went to Bethlehem (Matthew 1:18–25)? Research first-century marriage customs in Palestine.

15. What does Galatians 4:4 indicate about the timing of Christ's coming? What does David's statement in Psalm 31:15 tell us about the timing of events in our lives? What difference does this truth make in your ability to trust God when you don't understand what he is doing?

*"Born under the law..."*

*"My times are in your hands..."*

*It's encouraging... but still daunting when in the midst of "not knowing."*

 **Read Luke 2:21–38.**

## A MEANINGFUL BABY DEDICATION

The whole concept of God taking on human shape, and all the liturgy and ritual around that, had simply never made any sense to me. That was because, I realized one wonderful day, it was so simple. For people with bodies, important things like love have to be embodied. That's all. God had to be embodied, or else people with bodies would never in a trillion years understand about love.
—Jane Vonnegut Yarmolinsky
(*Angels Without Wings*, 116)

16. According to Jewish custom, when Jesus was forty days old, his parents traveled from Bethlehem to the temple in Jerusalem where they dedicated him to the Lord. What did Simeon say about Jesus (2:29–32)? What did Anna do (2:38)? How do you think Mary felt as she listened and watched?

- Destined for the falling and the rising of many in Israel – inner thoughts will be revealed – a sword will pierce your heart.

- Anna praised God – said child would redeem Jerusalem –

- Again, Mary must have felt supported and confirmed –

17. Simeon had specific words for Mary in verses 34 and 35. What did he say and what impact do you think these words had on her? Why do you think God spoke these words to Mary through Simeon? What was God doing?

*Warning Mary?*

DIGGING DEEPER

Mary's son was one of a kind. When Jesus was born, the part of the Godhead called the Son took human form and became a helpless baby. This event is often called "the humiliation." Why is this phrase appropriate? Study Philippians 2:5–11.

DIGGING DEEPER

Did the Son exist before he was born in human form in Bethlehem? Study John 1:1–2, 14; and John 8:58.

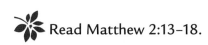 Read Matthew 2:13–18.

## ON THE ROAD AGAIN

18. At that time, King Herod ruled over Palestine. He heard about the arrival of a rival and instigated a murderous rampage to kill baby boys in Bethlehem and the surrounding area. How did God protect Jesus?

*Joseph was warned in a dream - Angel said to flee Egypt, king Herod was after Jesus*

19. Again, put yourself in Mary's shoes. What would this journey mean for Mary and her family? Would your trust in God have been shaken or strengthened by this unexpected detour to Egypt?

*I guess if Joseph had told me the dream I could understand that God was truly protecting Jesus. My faith would have been strengthened.*

20. After Herod died, the family returned to their homeland but not to Bethlehem in southern Israel near Jerusalem. To find out why, read Matthew 2:19–23. (*Note:* Archelaus was feared as an unstable tyrant, probably insane due to inbreeding [Walvoord and Zuck, *Bible Knowledge*, 23].) How did this move fulfill God's plan for Mary's son?

> They landed in Nazareth, fulfilling the prophecy that the Messiah would be a Nazorean.
> Joseph continues to have dreams of an angel telling him what to do —

DIGGING DEEPER

On a map, trace the routes Joseph, Mary, and young Jesus traveled. How far was their journey? What do you learn?

21. Can you relate to any of these circumstances: running from difficulty, moving constantly, adapting over and over to new situations? If so, please share how these experiences shaped you and your relationship with God.

 Read Luke 2:41–50.

## LOST

Our next glimpse of Jesus' family life comes through Luke when he records their trip to celebrate the Passover in Jerusalem when Jesus was twelve, the age a Jewish boy becomes a man. On their return trip home, his parents did not realize he was not with them until they had traveled some distance. They turned around and found their son in the temple, where he was interacting with the teachers of the Law, amazing everyone with his answers and insight.

22. His mother reacts differently from the teachers of the Law. What did she say in 2:48? How did Jesus respond (2:49)? How did Mary feel about his response (2:50)? Do you think this experience shook or strengthened her trust in God?

*2:48 "Why have you treated me so? Where so anxious."*

*2:49 "Why were you searching for me? Don't you know I need to be in my Father's house?"*

*2:50 Did not understand.*

*Maybe initially she was confused — but Jesus came home and was obedient and she "treasured" all these things in her heart.*

**Learning to Trust** (*3:38 minutes*). Are you one of those people who like to control everything in life? Hear how Sue learned—the hard way—to give up control and trust God.

23. Have you ever lost something precious? How did you react? What did you do? Can you identify the emotions that accompanied your reaction?

*Have lost pocket books — had to get credit cards cancelled, keys, lipstick, sun glasses, etc. Felt frustrated, angry at self for being careless, angry at others who stole...*

24. What special challenges did Mary face that are not typical of other mothers?

 Read Mark 3:20–21, 31–35.

## A FAMILY'S CONCERN

25. Jesus left home to begin his three-year ministry prior to the cross. What happened in Mark 3:20 that concerned his family? How might you feel if you heard that a loved one was not taking good care of himself? What did the family determine to do (3:21)? *They tried to restrain Jesus. Would have done the same!*

26. Mary and Jesus' brothers tracked him down to bring him home. When they found him, he was teaching a crowd of people, probably in a home. Rather than barge in, what did his family do there (3:31–32)? *They stood outside and sent someone into the crowd to reach Jesus*

27. How did Jesus respond (3:33–34)?

*He said all were his brothers, mother and sister who did the will of God.*

28. Can you "read between the lines" and discern what Jesus was saying to Mary? How do you think Mary felt as she processed Jesus' reply? Why do you think Jesus did not return home with his mother?

*His ministry had begun. Hopefully Mary began to understand.*

29. Compare verses 33 and 35. Who did Jesus include in verse 35 who was not mentioned in verse 33? Why is this inclusion significant—maybe especially for Mary? How was her role changing?

*35 – sisters – ~~not that mother~~.*

*As of all adult children, mothers have a different role – need to let them go!*

30. Can you recall a time when you were forced to relinquish control and
    entrust a loved one or difficult situation to God? If so, please share the
    situation and what you learned.

    *Yes! Had no choice — could not control
    the situation —*

31. After the occasion in Mark 3, the next time a gospel writer tells us
    about the relationship between Jesus and Mary is at the cross. *Read
    John 19:25–27.* Imagine how Mary must have been feeling as she saw
    her precious son suspended in agony. What did Jesus say to her to show
    that she still occupied a special place in his heart?

    *"Woman, here's your son — and to his disciple
    he said she is your mother too — and the
    beloved disciple took her home up there."*

## A NEW ROLE

32. Jesus died, was resurrected, and forty days later ascended to God the
    Father (Acts 1:3–11). *Read Acts 1:12–14.* After the disciples witnessed
    his ascension, they returned to Jerusalem to wait for the "gift" of the
    Holy Spirit that Jesus promised. Who was there to wait and pray with
    them (1:14)?

    *Certain women, Mary, the mother; as well
    as his brothers —*

33. Mary's role changed from mother to disciple, a journey of trust, doubt, pain, distance, and ultimately renewed trust and worship. She had sacrificed much for him when he was little. She was undoubtedly sometimes perplexed as she raised this one-of-a-kind son. When he was an adult, she was forced to relinquish control over his life, as she watched him slandered, mistreated, and finally crucified. But she also witnessed his exoneration. What have you learned about Mary that will help you on your journey?

*To hold fast ...*

## PROMISES

34. *Read Psalm 27:7–14.* What has Jesus promised Mary and all who follow him that helps us to trust God in our journey through trials and triumphs?

*" Wait for the Lord; be strong, and let your heart take courage; wait for the Lord."*

Sometimes we see God more clearly in the dark, when he has our undistracted attention and we struggle to know if the hand that rules the night is as good and powerful as the hand that rules the day.
—Carolyn Custis James
(*When Life*, 89)

35. *Read John 14:1–3 and Revelation 21:1–4.* Why should we trust Jesus, relinquishing control to him? What kind of future is Jesus preparing for Mary and all who follow him?

• In my father's house are many mansions — will prepare a place for you — all we have to do is follow him —

• A new heaven and a new earth — no pain, no death!

36. Pen a note to Mary, expressing what you have learned from her life. What do you plan to say to her when you meet her in eternity?

To thank her for being brave enough to go along w/ what she'd been asked to do — and to have been such an example of trusting God yet not knowing how it would all play out. I would tell her how much I identified w/ her concern for her son's well being and w/ the agony she must have felt when Christ was crucified. I would love to know how much she really understood about Jesus. Did she "get" what he was proclaiming? Did the rest of the family?

I'm glad that Jesus, even while on the cross, made certain that she would be cared for — and wonder where Joseph was ...

So, I guess, after thanking her, I would have lots of questions for her!

# Swap Fear for Faith

## *The Widow of Nain*

**OPTIONAL**

Memorize 1 John 4:18

There is no fear in love. But perfect love drives out fear, because fear has to do with punishment. The one who fears is not made perfect in love.

A car rear-ends you on the freeway; you get a pink slip or a bad mammogram report; you find lipstick that is not your shade on your husband's collar; you make a 911 call and they can't help; or, in the case of the people in our lesson, a valued servant is dying and a beloved son has died. Unexpected events strike fear into our hearts. Our pulses race, hands shake, heads pound.

> [Aunt Edith] was coming home from a neighbor's house one Saturday afternoon. As she came nearer to the house she saw her five youngest children huddled together and preoccupied with something of great interest. After some minutes of trying to discover the center of the attraction, she came close enough to see they were playing with baby skunks! Aghast, she cried at the top of her voice, "Children, run!" At which point each child picked up a skunk and ran! Isn't that exactly what we do with our burdens and cares? . . . we hug them so close that the smell of them clings to us. (Haggai, *How to Win Over Worry*, 176–77)

Life is full of unexpected surprises, sometimes more pungent than the temporary smell of skunk spray. Does God know? Does he even care? Let's find out.

 **Read Luke 7:1–10.**

Capernaum was a fishing village located on the northern shore of the Sea of Galilee. It was the hometown of four of Jesus' disciples—Peter, James, John, and Matthew. Jesus chose this town to be the center of his public ministry before he made his way south to Jerusalem to face the cross. Today, in Capernaum, you can visit the ruins of an ancient synagogue, an early Christian church, and even the place tradition claims is Peter's home. Under the excavated synagogue that you can view is an older, still buried synagogue, probably built by the centurion in our lesson. If you have the opportunity to travel to Israel, take it; it will bring the Bible alive!   —Sue

DIGGING DEEPER

Consult a Bible dictionary to learn all you can about centurions. How does this information enrich the account?

The word for *servant* in the original language is the same as the word *slave*. Some worked as domestics, barbers, butlers, cooks, hairdressers, maids, nurses, secretaries, and seamstresses. However, the brightest were trained to serve as professionals in fields like accounting, education, and medicine. Statistics vary but it's estimated that as many as 20 percent of people in the Roman Empire were slaves.

# A DARK DAY FOR A ROMAN CENTURION

1. Why was this a dark day for the Roman centurion? Why might he have been afraid? What was his plan (7:3)?

   *A valued slave was ill and dying. He wasn't Jewish — appealed to Jewish elders to approach Jesus for him.*

2. According to the Jewish elders, why should Jesus heal the centurion's servant (7:4–5)? Who, in their estimation, is worthy of God's favor?

   *The centurion likes Jews — built them a synagogue.*
   *Someone who earns God's favor.*

3. What does the centurion say about himself (7:6–7)? What does this reveal about the difference in the elders' and the centurion's attitudes toward God?

   *The centurion, though powerful by worldly standards, believes that he may not please God, that he's unworthy of favor he's asking of Jesus.*

4. The centurion commanded many soldiers. As a result, what did he understand about Jesus (7:8)?

"I am also a man set under authority..." that Jesus had power to —

5. What amazed Jesus about the centurion's response? What did Jesus say to the crowd about the centurion (7:9)? What do you think he was attempting to teach the crowd?

The centurion said that he knew Jesus only needed to speak to heal. Jesus praise & his faith — and commented that even in Israel there was not such faith.

These are the only two occasions on which we have the statement that Jesus marveled [the NIV uses the word *amazed*]. Once at unbelief, and once at belief, He marveled. The statement that He marveled does not mean that He was ignorant, but rather that He had clear comprehension of that man's faith, of the majesty of it, of the sweep of it, of the grasp of it, of the marvel of it.
—G. Campbell Morgan
(*Gospel*, 95)

In the case of the centurion and his servant, notice that Jesus responded to the request of one person on behalf of another. It's OK to pray for others and to ask them to pray for you. —Sue

6. How did Jesus minister to the centurion (7:10)?

The slave was made well.

7. Do you know anyone today whom you would call a man or woman of great faith? If so, why?

*Yes — actually I know many. They live faithfully.*

8. What one change can you make in your life right now to become a woman of greater faith?

*- To take each day as it comes and be fully present in it. To be glad in it trusting that God will be of me in the future — as well as present daily.*
*- To be more consistent of my quiet time, to pray more.*

 Read Luke 7:11–17.

## A DARK DAY FOR A JEWISH WIDOW

9. From Capernaum and his encounter with the centurion, Jesus traveled to Nain, a twenty-five-mile walk. Who came with him (7:11)? In your opinion, why?

*His disciples — and a lrg. crowd*
*Everyone wanted to hear more, see more.*

10. As they approached the town gate, what did they see (7:12)?

*The son of a widow had died and was being carried out — was the only son of this widow.*

11. How did Jesus respond to the sight (7:13)?

*Jesus felt compassion for the widow and brought the son to life again —*

12. Because of the structure of Jewish society, women were totally dependent on men—fathers, husbands, sons, or brothers. Without a close male relative, females usually lacked security, support, and resources. Many were mistreated and destitute. Put yourself in this widow's shoes. How would you respond to the difficult and life-altering circumstance of an only son's death?

*Would have to learn a trade, depend on friends — pray a lot!*

Justice seeks out only the *merits* of the case, but pity only regards the *need*.
—Bernard of Clairvaux
(Wiersbe, *Be Compassionate*, 89)

---❀---

Jesus always talked to the dead as if they were alive, because even though their body was dead, their spirit was alive. Consider the implications. —Sue

Compassion has been defined as "your pain in my heart."
—Warren Wiersbe
(*Be Compassionate*, 89)

13. What is God's attitude toward widows? What had God commanded the Jews to do for the less fortunate (Deuteronomy 10:17–19; 27:19)? If you are a widow, please share your experiences to help others be more sensitive and supportive.

*God wants them to be treated well, to be cared for*

14. How did the Jewish leaders treat widows (Luke 20:47)?

*They devore widow's houses!*

15. In contrast, what did Jesus do to help the widow in Nain (7:13–15)? Describe the scene.

*He comforted her, brought her back to life. The crowd was at first frightened. Then praised Jesus.*

16. In the process, Jesus probably offended the Jewish leaders by touching the coffin (Leviticus 21:10–12). Was it necessary for Jesus to touch the coffin to heal the son? Consider how Jesus healed the centurion's servant. Why do you think Jesus chose to work this miracle this way?

*Maybe to show there was now a new order – that no one is untouchable.*

17. Reread Luke 7:16–17. How did the people there react? What did they learn about Jesus that day?

*That he was at least a prophet –*

## CONTRASTS AND COMPARISONS

Take a deeper look into the miracles for the centurion and the widow.

18. Consider the social status, ethnicity, and gender of the centurion and the widow. What does this tell you about God?

*God cares for all people –*

19. According to Luke's account, on what basis did the widow "deserve" Jesus' help? On what basis did the Jews say the centurion deserved Jesus' help? What does this tell you about God?

The widow was in great need — as was the centurion. The Jews would probably felt the widow deserved nothing ... just the way things are. They felt the centurion deserved help because he was a friend and built their synagogue. God has compassion for all people

20. Contrast the faith of the centurion with the faith of the widow. What does this tell you about God?

Sometimes a show of faith is not necessary.

21. Do you think the widow came to faith after Jesus raised her son from the dead? Explain your reasoning.

I would certainly hope so! He demonstrated great love for her.

22. Who merits the grace of God? What should be the normal response when one receives his grace?

*No one merits the grace of God. It's a gift for all.*

23. Jesus constantly pointed out that one of the great flaws of the Jewish leaders was their arrogant attitudes—especially toward people of other races, classes, and gender. Why do you think he chose to work these two particular miracles back to back for these two very different people and onlookers? Summarize what they had in common and how they were different. What is the lesson for us today?

*One was not a Jew and the other was a woman, Jewish, who would need help to live – was not valued.*

*We need to look at people through God's eyes.*

To live with fear and not be afraid is the final test of maturity.

—Edward Weeks

24. When was the last time you were afraid? What happened and how did you respond?

*felt ill — took care of it w/ medical care.*

**Fearful** (*3:43 minutes*). No matter how fear-filled your life has been, God can help you overcome.

Fear paralyzes us. It causes ambition and courage to leak out and leaves us without resources to face even the simplest situations.

—Vickie Kraft
(*Facing Your Feelings*, 57)

25. Make a list of your fears in order of degree. Analyze the list. What can you learn about yourself?

*Lee's health
our immediate family's cohesion.
old age/care
children's mistakes
Nation's political scene
my health
children's love & faith*

26. *Read 1 John 4:18*. What do you think John was attempting to tell us? Paraphrase the verse.

*There is no fear in perfect love! That is love of God - and others, all others.*

Perfect love drives out fear.
—1 John 4:18

27. Isaiah was an unpopular prophet called to deliver a hard message to Israel, a message they did not want to hear or obey. They ignored his warnings and, as a result, the Jews were taken into Babylon as exiles and the land was left desolate. Even so, what was God's message to them and to us in Isaiah 43:1–3a?

*Redemption is promised —*

28. Do the promises in Isaiah 43:1–3a mean that nothing bad will ever happen to you? What is God promising in order to help you turn fear into faith?

*Obviously. The Holocaust proved that in recent times. The promise is that God will be w/ us even in hazardous times.*

Do not be afraid of those who kill the body and after that can do no more. But I will show you whom you should fear: Fear him who, after your body has been killed, has authority to throw you into hell. . . . Are not five sparrows sold for two pennies? Yet not one of them is forgotten by God. Indeed, the very hairs of your head are all numbered. Don't be afraid; you are worth more than many sparrows.
—Jesus (Luke 12:4–7)

29. "Wring out" the following passages. What specific situations do these verses address? What do you observe that can help you turn fear into faith?

Psalm 23:4

Even walking thru the valley of death — or the darkest valley, God will be of me and comfort me.

Psalm 91:1–6

Assurance of God's protection

Proverbs 1:32–33

" Those who listen to me will be secure and will live at ease, w/out dread of disaster."

Proverbs 31:21

" She is not afraid for her household... for all her household are clothed in scarlet. a women's domain is valued!

Isaiah 35:4

God will come and save you. And deal of those who hurt us.

Isaiah 41:10

God will strengthen us, will help us

30. Quickly review the two miracles in Luke 7:1–17. Summarize what you gleaned to help you fight fear with faith.

*That even when we don't ask for help, God has compassion for us / for all people.*

31. Pen a note to the widow of Nain, expressing what you learned from this incident in her life. What do you plan to say to her when you meet her in eternity?

• *That Jesus took pity on you is an encouragement to me that Jesus would care for me too.*

• *Would want to know how her faith changed after her son was raised — how her life changed, how others treated her.*

### If Only I Had Known You

Lord,
I crawled
  across the barrenness
    to You
      with my empty cup
  uncertain
  in asking
  any small drop
Of refreshment.

If only
I had known You
    better
I'd have come
Running
With a bucket.

—Nancy Spiegelberg © 1974

# Tame Sin with Gratitude

## The "Wild" Woman

H ave you ever forgotten that God forgets your sins? Maybe you think your sins are so grotesque that they are unforgivable? The ghost of these blacklist sins haunts you from time to time. Or maybe you keep repeating the same sin over and over, even when you promised Jesus you would stop.

> I was thanking the Father today for his mercy. I began listing the sins he'd forgiven. One by one I thanked God for forgiving my stumbles and tumbles. My motives were pure and my heart was thankful, but my understanding of God was wrong. It was when I used the word *remember* that it hit me.
>
> "Remember the time I . . ." I was about to thank God for another act of mercy. But I stopped. Something was wrong. The word *remember* seemed displaced. It was an off-key in a sonata, a misspelled word in a poem. It was a baseball game in December. It didn't fit. "Does he remember?"
>
> Then *I* remembered. I remembered his words, "And I will remember their sins no more."
>
> Wow! Now *that* is a remarkable promise. (Lucado, *God Came Near*, 101)

Luke included an account of Jesus' interaction with a sinful woman to help us find truth, hope, and healing as we deal with sin.

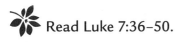 Read Luke 7:36–50.

**OPTIONAL**

Memorize Ephesians 2:4–5

Because of his great love for us, God, who is rich in mercy, made us alive with Christ even when we were dead in transgressions—it is by grace you have been saved.

To forgive means to release others from a debt incurred when they wronged us. The debt may be material or emotional, some form of hurt or embarrassment. When we forgive, we assume the loss. We free others from the bondage of material or emotional indebtedness. If we refuse to forgive, we place ourselves in bondage to an unforgiving spirit, which is accompanied by tension, strife, pressure, irritation, frustration, and anxiety.
—Charles Stanley
(*Gift of Forgiveness*, 85)

In first-century Israel, most living areas were small, so when weather allowed, daily living—including entertaining—occurred outside on patios and even on rooftops. Thus it was not unusual for outsiders to hover around during these parties to watch "important people" and overhear their conversations. It was even possible for them to enter from the street and speak to a guest.

After healing the Roman centurion's servant and raising the widow's son from the dead, Jesus was the talk of the town. A Jewish leader named Simon decided it was time to meet this up-and-coming rabbi, so he invited him to a dinner party.

Imagine dinner on the veranda at the home of a wealthy and prominent community leader. Passersby drink in delicious smells and wish for an invitation. Selected guests arrive and are greeted with courtesies appropriate for their station in life—a kiss on the cheek, a bit of oil on the head, some water to wash away the dust from the street. All are honored with these Eastern tokens of respect—except one.

It's probably a warm night because the guests are outside reclining on sofas, sprawled out on their sides like wheel spokes around a central table, sharing delicacies.

1. Imagine the scene. From Luke 7:37, answer the following questions:

- Who interrupted their meal?

  *"Sinful" woman — had not been invited*

According to the customs of the time, women were not invited to banquets. Jewish rabbis did not speak to women in public nor would they eat with them there. A woman of this type would certainly not be welcomed in the house of a Pharisee.

- What kind of woman was she?

  *Sinful*

- What did she bring?

  *perfume*

Before this event, Jesus had been teaching and healing constantly in that area of the country. Perhaps this woman heard his gracious invitation, "Come to me . . . and I will give you rest," and responded, turning from her life of sin and shame, and trusting Jesus as her Savior. Her tears, humble heart, and expensive alabaster perfume jar all speak of her overwhelming love and gratitude.  —Sue

2. Why do you think she was weeping (7:38)?

   *Apparently she had heard of the message of Jesus — was in need of the healing she needed.*

3. Remember that Jesus' feet were still dirty. What did she do with the vase she brought (7:38)? What did this act communicate?

*She anointed his feet with the perfume — She had deep respect for him —*

4. First-century Jewish women did not allow anyone outside their families to see them with loosened hair (Mathews, *A Woman God Can Lead*, 296). In order to wipe Jesus' feet with her hair, she needed to let down her locks. What do you think led her to this bold act?

*She was humbling herself, being totally vulnerable.*

## THE HOST RESPONDS

5. Simon was watching Jesus to discern if he was really sent from God. What was his conclusion as he watched the sinful woman massage Jesus' feet (7:39)?

*Felt that Jesus was not a prophet — would have known the woman was a sinner — and sent her away from him.*

We are like beasts when we kill. We are like men when we judge. We are like God when we forgive.
—William Arthur Ward
(McKenzie, *14,000 Quips*, 188)

6. What was one attribute of a prophet that Simon was looking for (7:39)?

*Could see a person's wrongdoing —*

7. How do you think Simon expected a prophet of God to act?

*Would reward the righteous, the most religious, the law keepers.*

## A STORY FOR THE DINNER GUESTS

Once President Lincoln was asked how he was going to treat the rebellious southerners when they had finally been defeated and returned to the Union of the United States. The questioner expected that Lincoln would take a dire vengeance, but he answered, "I will treat them as if they had never been away."
—William Barclay
(*Gospel of Luke*, 244)

8. Knowing Simon's thoughts, Jesus told him a story that ended with a question (7:40–42). (*Note:* A denarius was a coin worth about a day's wages.) Paraphrase the story in modern-day language.

*$500.00 vs. fifty dollars —*

9. How would you answer the question at the end of the story? How did Simon answer?

*The same — The one who owed the most was the most grateful —*

10. In Jesus' story, who represented the one who owed five hundred denarii? Who represented the one who owed fifty? ,

*• Those q us who have sinned most — the ones who have broken rules q society and the religious.*

*• Those who have tried to be faithful as they knew to be —*

11. Why is it important that neither borrower could pay back the money-lender, regardless of the amount owed?

*all are in need of forgiveness ! and grace.*

12. What do you think was the main point of the story?

> Those who truly repent and experience God's forgiveness feel great relief and gratitude.

## A GUEST'S REBUKE

13. From verses 44–46, name the three ways Simon was rude to Jesus when he arrived. Then name the three ways the sinful woman fulfilled these courtesies.

> • Did not wash his ft.
> - " " kiss him
> - " " anoint head w/ oil

14. What was the woman expressing through these extravagant courtesies?

> Her deep gratitude

15. Just as Jesus could read Simon's thoughts and knew his heart, what do you think Jesus also knew about this woman's heart?

*He was aware of her need and her faith in him —*

16. What did Jesus announce publicly about this sinful woman (7:47)? How do you think she felt at that moment?

*Her sins are forgiven - for she loves greatly-*
*joyous -*

17. Then Jesus turned to the woman and spoke. What did he say to her (7:48)? Why do you think a public announcement was not enough? What does this reveal about Jesus?

*Your sins are have been forgiven. Being personally addressed showed that he regarded her as important, someone worthy of his attention*

**Corrie's Story** (*4:49 minutes*). We can learn so much from the story of one faithful, courageous woman.

## ONLY GOD CAN FORGIVE SINS

If you are suffering from a
bad man's injustice, forgive
him lest there be two bad
men.

—Augustine
(McKenzie,
*14,000 Quips*, 143)

18. How did the other guests react (7:49)?

*who is this man who can forgive sins?*

19. On what basis was the sinful woman redeemed (7:50; see also 1 John 5:5)?

- *Her faith —*
- *That Jesus is the son of God —*

We must not conclude that
this woman was saved by her
tears and her gift. Jesus made
it clear that . . . no amount
of good works can pay for
salvation (Titus 3:4–7). Nor
should we think that lost sinners are saved by love, either
God's love for them or their
love for God. God loves the
whole world (John 3:16), yet
the whole world is not saved.
"For by grace you have been
saved through faith, and that
not of yourselves; it is the gift
of God, not of works, lest
anyone should boast" (Eph.
2:8–9 NKJV).

—Warren Wiersbe
(*Be Compassionate*, 97–98)

20. Simon looked down with disgust on this woman because he consid-
    ered her to be "a sinner" (Luke 7:39). What was he forgetting about
    himself (7:42)?

    *That he was also a sinner!*

21. How was his sin different from hers? Why was she forgiven and he was not?

*I thought he was better than others — certainly better than the woman. He still did not "know" Jesus. — did not ask for forgiveness.*

 Read Mark 2:1–12.

## PROVE IT!

It's one thing to say "your sins are forgiven" and another to actually *show* that you have the power to forgive sins. Early in his ministry Jesus worked this miracle to authenticate the truth that he could, indeed, forgive sins.

22. Four friends were sure that Jesus could heal their paralyzed companion. What did they do to express their faith (Mark 2:1–4)?

*They went to a lot of trouble to get their companion close to Jesus.*

Due to Israel's mild climate, peoples' rooftops served as an extension of the home, often cooled by sea breezes. Roofs of simple homes were constructed in three layers: The first was wooden beams, often cypress and sometimes cedar. On top of the beams, straw mats were laid, and on top of these, a layer of clay. The clay would be packed down tight each year before the winter rains, using a stone roller. More expensive homes were roofed with tiles.

23. What did Jesus say to their friend before he healed him (2:5)?

*Your sins are forgiven*

24. What were the Jewish leaders thinking as they listened (2:6–7)?

*who but God can forgive sins? This man blasphemes.*

25. How did Jesus show everyone there that he did have the power to forgive sins (2:8–12)? How would you answer Jesus' question in verse 9?

*He enabled the man to walk - to be healed.*

DIGGING DEEPER

Wring out Ephesians 2:1–10. What amazing truths are revealed in this passage that help us understand God's power to forgive sins? What is your response?

26. Who alone can cancel our debt of sin? How does this work (see Romans 5:6–11)?

*Christ - who died for all of us - so that we could be reconciled w/ Him and w/ each other.*

27. *Read Psalm 103:10–13.* What do you learn about the transgressions of the "wild" woman (Luke 7:36–50) and our sins, too?

*That we are not dealt according to our sins, nor recorded according to our iniquities — removes transgressions across the board.*

28. Can you recall a time when you brought your sin to Jesus and experienced forgiveness as he covered you with his righteousness? If so, describe your response to his amazing grace.

You have been damaged. But you have great hope. The mercy of God does not eradicate the damage, at least not in this life, but it soothes the soul and draws it forward to a hope that purifies and sets free. Allow the pain of the past and the travail of the change process to create fresh new life in you and to serve as a bridge over which another victim may walk from death to life.
—Dan Allender
(*Wounded Heart*, 57)

Satan knows the hardest person for us to forgive will always be ourself.
—Beth Moore (*Get Out*, 37)

*"Everyone who believes in him receives forgiveness of sins through his name" (Acts 10:43). If you have never taken that step of faith, won't you consider doing so now? Jesus loves you dearly and waits to cleanse you and give you a new start. If you struggle to trust him, that's OK. Keep seeking.*

29. What is the only sin that Jesus will not forgive (Mark 3:28–29)? What does this mean?

*Whoever blasphemes the Holy Spirit —*

DIGGING DEEPER

Study Galatians 3:1–5. Why was Paul irritated at the Galatians? How does his rebuke relate to our study this week?

DIGGING DEEPER

Chart and study Romans 6:1–18 to discover theological truths about our new life in Christ.

30. If you are a Christian, what power do your past sins have over you (Rom. 8:31–39)?

*They cannot separate you from God's love —*

31. Simon did not think of himself as a sinner. What did Paul say to people who think like that (Romans 3:10)?

*"There is none righteous, not even one."*

32. Name the sins you think women in your church or neighborhood have committed. (No names, please.) What is your attitude toward "sinful" women? Have you ever thought or acted like the Jewish leader?

33. Do you think the sinful woman cleaned up her act? If so, why? What is the greatest motivation for leaving sin and living a better life?

*Watching close to Jesus, wanting to be more and more like him —*

Thanklessness keeps bad, bad company. It is a mood, a state of mind and soul. . . . You cannot be well or enjoy good health when this moral virus is encouraged and rampant in your being.
—C. M. Ward (*Sermons*, 78)

View your past failures as reminders of God's grace. Your past sins should become memorials to the grace of God in your life. When Satan accuses you of being unworthy . . . you can respond by saying (and I recommend actually speaking out loud), "That is exactly right. I did do that, and that's not all. But before I ever committed my first sin Jesus Christ died and paid for my sins."
—Charles Stanley (*Gift of Forgiveness*, 54)

34. Is gaining power over sin a one-time act or a process? What would you say to the "wild" woman the first time she slipped back into some of her old habits?

*To keep forgiving herself — and to keep on becoming more Christ like.*

35. Do you struggle to forgive yourself of past or continuing sin? Your sins are no worse than those of the "sinful" woman. What one thing can you do this week to remember that Jesus forgets our sins? What one thing can you do to eradicate one particular sin from your life?

*The sin that plagues me is very difficult in living — and forgiveness — those who hurt me —*

36. Pen a note to the "wild" woman, expressing what you have learned from her life. What do you plan to say to her when you meet her in eternity?

*I'm glad to see you here! Good to see ya!!*

**Beginning Anew**

He came to my desk with quivering lip; the lesson was
    done . . .
"Have you a new leaf for me, dear Teacher? I have spoiled
    this one!"
I took his leaf, all soiled and blotted, and gave him a new
    one, all unspotted;
Then into his tired heart I smiled: "Do better now, my
    child."

I went to the throne with trembling heart; the day was
    done.
"Have you a new one for me, dear Master? I have spoiled
    this one!"
He took my day, all soiled and blotted, and gave me a new
    one, all unspotted;
Then into my tired heart He smiled: "Do better now, my
    child."

—Kathleen Wheeler (Rice, Poems That Preach)

# Trade Silence or Aggression for a Beautiful Voice

## *Lessons from Three Women*

OPTIONAL

Memorize Proverbs 15:23

A person finds joy in giving an apt reply—and how good is a timely word!

I teach seminary classes, both mixed-gender and all female. In the mixed-gender classes, women students are quieter, but these same students participate heartily in my all-women courses. I see the same phenomenon in Sunday school. Many women speak up less when men are present. Why? Do these women feel excluded or intimidated? What shuts them down?

> Many women, for a variety of reasons, are indirect in spelling out what they need or want. For example, of the graduates of Carnegie Mellon University with a master's degree in a business-related field, male graduates earn, on average, 8 percent more than female graduates. But why? Research shows that the men asked for more money. During the job-finding process only 7 percent of the women asked for a larger salary compared to 57 percent of the men. The gender gap in salary would have closed if the women had only asked. (Edwards, Mathews, and Rogers, *Mixed Ministry*, 1–2)

On the other extreme, I observe bulldozer women speaking up too much, in hostile tones, or inappropriately. How we communicate matters. We reveal who we are and we gain influence through our voices. How do you think Jesus feels about our voices and the way we use them? Let's find out.

 Read Luke 8:40–56.

## A LOUD PLEA FROM A DESPERATE FATHER

1. Who pleaded for Jesus' help and why (Luke 8:40–42)? Describe the scene. *Jairus, a leader of the synagogue — wanted healing for his 12-yr-daughter. There was a crowd of people — all welcoming Jesus.*

2. How old was the ailing girl? What was the social status of the family? What do you think the townspeople probably thought of her?

   • *12 yrs.*
   - *probably high social status*
   - *felt favorably toward her*

## A SILENT PLEA FROM A DESPERATE WOMAN

3. What happened to deter Jesus from reaching Jairus's daughter (8:42b–43)? How do you think Jairus was feeling during the delay? *An hemorrhous woman touched Jesus' garment for healing.*

   *Jairus was probably anxious, irritable even angry.*

Twelve years! While we aren't positive what this bleeding was, it is usually assumed that it was a continuous menstrual period—for twelve long years. Even in today's world with modern medicine to help us, that would be exhausting and debilitating. As for any modern woman today, for her it would have meant being sapped of energy. It meant constant suffering and weakness. . . . But in the time of Jesus it was much, much worse. To begin with, her bleeding made her a social outcast. . . . Women with flows of blood were ritually unclean, literally untouchable. . . . She could not maintain a normal relationship. She would be cut off from all good Jews both male and female. . . . She was isolated from all community life, avoided, excluded. She was shut off from the corporate worship of God. If she brushed up against a shopkeeper, he was defiled. . . . People assumed she was being punished by God for some secret sin. She was probably excommunicated, divorced, and ostracized. . . . But she heard Jesus was in town. A flicker of hope. (Mathews, *A Woman God Can Lead*, 269–72)

4. The woman had been bleeding as long as Jairus's daughter had been alive. Contrast the lives of these two females.

- One was an outcast.
- One was cherished

5. In her desperation, what did the woman do? What happened as a result (8:44)?

She touched the garment that Jesus wore - and he felt it.
Immediately the woman's bleeding stopped!

In English, verse 44 reads, "She came up behind him and touched the edge of his cloak," but the word "touched" does not accurately convey the meaning of the Greek word. A better translation would be "clutched." She fastened upon his garment, but not the hem or border as the English translation portrays. She grasped the *kraspedon*, the tassel of his prayer shawl. Numbers 15 describes how these prayer shawls were to be made and worn. The purpose was to remind the wearer of God's commandments as he went about his day. Threads of blue were woven into these tassels, and one of the tassels was always at the back of the wearer as he walked along. The woman clutched Jesus' tassel in desperation.

6. Jesus stopped and addressed the crowd. What did he say (8:46)?

*He said he knew someone had touched him – noticed power had gone out from him.*

7. Do you think Jesus really knew who touched him? If so, why did he ask the question?

*Probably – Maybe wanted others to hear her story as an example of faith healing and to have her acknowledge that she was healed.*

8. Why do you think this woman preferred to remain silent and anonymous at first (8:47a)? How do you think she was probably feeling?

*Was afraid — but hopeful.*

Once when I was speaking in a webinar, the host did a poll of the women participating, asking the question, "Do you hold back your voice so that men are more comfortable with your gifting?" Sixty-eight percent of the women said they did. Now some of that *holding back* may be wise to overcome possible misconceptions and male concerns that women may be too domineering. But some women may not speak up out of insecurity, fear, or uncertainty. For most women, figuring out when to speak and how to express ourselves in a mixed-gender group is complicated. —Sue

9. Why do you think Jesus called attention to her, insisting that she speak up, confess her faith, and declare what he had done for her (8:47)?

*To become an example for others — All can be healed and made whole.*

---

 **Find Your Voice** (*4:47 minutes*). When it's time to speak up for Christ, are you tongue-tied? Sue shares a time when she "lost her voice," and what she learned from it.

---

10. What do you think she would have done if he had not called her out of the shadows?

*Maybe tell her family — as a member of a synagogue…*

11. Have you observed women who tend to remain silent when God is calling them to speak up and tell others who he is and what he has done for them? If so, why do you think this is typical of some women?

12. Do you tend to remain silent when God is calling you to speak up? If so, can you discern why?

It is hard for me to "witness" — don't want to be ridiculed, dismissed as "pushy", to share", pious, etc

13. In your opinion, what causes some women to lose their voice at critical times? Enumerate as many reasons as you can. What can we do to help women learn to speak up when God nudges them to communicate for him?

- lack of coming on too strong
- fear of being misunderstood
- " " that what they say doesn't matter, that no one is listening.
- fear they might hurt feelings, make matters worse.
- fear that what they already went will be ignored.
- fear that they will appear to be uninformed or stupid
- " " that they will be punished, reprimanded.

14. Was Jesus pleased with her words? How did he address her as he left? Why would this term be important, considering the past twelve years? How would her life be different now? What did he wish for her as he left (8:48)? (Note: The Greek text actually says, "Go into peace.")

Yes! "Daughter, your faith has made you well; go in peace."
She was no longer an outcast, an adventity. Her anguish was over.

We dilute the beauty of the gospel story when we divorce it from our lives, our worlds, the words and images that God is writing now on our souls.

—Shauna Niequist
(Bittersweet, 239)

15. Jesus said to the woman, "Daughter, your faith has healed you." Did
    her faith heal her? Ponder the statement, "It is the object of one's faith
    and not the amount of one's faith that makes the difference." What
    actually healed the woman?

    *She touched Jesus's garment — she
    had faith in him.*

## A SECOND MIRACLE

16. Meanwhile, what happened at Jairus's home (8:49)? What did Jesus tell
    Jairus? Briefly, what happened (8:50–56)? (*Note:* Jairus exhibited faith
    in Christ when he allowed Jesus to enter his home right after he had
    been touched by an unclean woman.)

    *The 12 yr. old girl died — when Jesus
    heard this he told Jairus not to
    worry — that the girl was just asleep.
    Jesus took the girl by the hand and
    said, "Child, get up." Her spirit
    returned and she got up immediately.
    He told the family to get her something
    to eat!*

 Read Matthew 20:20–24.

## A FOOLISH REQUEST

17. The mother of James and John (the sons of Zebedee) came to Jesus with a request. What was it? What was their posture? (Matthew 20:20–21)

    _She wanted special favors for her sons – that they be elevated to stand beside Jesus._

When communicating, I needed to learn the difference between assertion and aggression. That distinction made all the difference in my effectiveness working with both men and women. To assert means to state or declare positively, with God-confidence, with assurance, to be direct but gracious. To be aggressive means to come into a conversation with an edge, to attack, to display a militant or combative attitude. As a woman, I stand a far better chance of earning a hearing and being treated with respect if I approach others with an assertive attitude rather than an aggressive one. I've yet to see a man respond well to aggression.   —Sue

18. Because the "you" in Jesus' response is plural, we know that Jesus did not respond to her but to James and John instead. What did Jesus say to them (20:22–23)? What do you think he meant?

    _Are you ready for any trial in following me? Even to suffer? Place where one sits by Jesus in his kingdom is for God alone to know._

The tongue has the power of life and death, and those who love it will eat its fruit.
    —Proverbs 18:21

19. How do you suppose Jesus received this request? Why do you think he responded to his disciples while ignoring their mother?

> *Rather than ignoring the mother, addressed the sons because they were the ones who had the speak for them.*

20. How did the other apostles react when they heard about this request (20:24)? Do you think Jesus shared in their sentiments? If so, why?

> *"Angry –*
> *• No – understood their reasoning – wanted to be great rulers – but there will be no hierarchy – all will be servants*

21. Have you experienced a woman using an aggressive communication style that backfired? If so, what do you think might have been her motivation? (No names, please.) Have you tried this yourself? If so, elaborate.

Read Mark 7:24–30.

## THE WOMAN WHO GOT IT RIGHT!

On one occasion, Jesus traveled outside Palestine and into Gentile territory to Tyre, modern-day Lebanon. He was not there to minister publicly but to secure private time to instruct his disciples. But the news of his arrival leaked out and a desperate mother found him, fell at his feet, and directly requested that he heal her daughter (Mark 7:24–26).

22. How did Jesus answer her request (7:27)? How do you think she probably felt?

"Let the children be fed 1st... not fair to take the children's food and throw it to the dogs".

The woman had a good response - was not exterminated

23. Have you ever gone to a man with a request, perhaps a male boss or ministry leader, and been turned down? If so, how did you feel? What was your response?

Hope for the theologian is also in the very real and often painful present where the pieces do not fit neatly together and agonizing questions about Jesus will not go away.

—Carolyn Custis James (*When Life*, 229)

24. This Gentile woman would not allow Jesus' answer to deter her. She knew her cause was worthy. Instead, how did she reply (7:28)? Do you think her response was wise or foolish?

> Wise — Even the dogs eat the crumbs of the children...
> Even a morsel of Jesus's compassion was enough to heal her child.

25. Did Jesus think her response was wise or foolish? What did he say and what did she find when she arrived home (7:29–30)? Why do you think he granted her request?

> He approved — even said it was the reason her daughter would be healed — and she was!

## FIND YOUR VOICE

26. Think back over the communication styles of the bleeding woman, the mother of James and John, and the Gentile woman. Compare and contrast how they used words for good or ill.

27. One woman was tongue-tied, another aggressive, and another asser-
    tive. What are *your* definitions of *aggression* and *assertion*? In your opin-
    ion, which woman in our lesson fits which term?

28. Is your communication style similar to any of these three women? If
    so, which one? Can you discern why?

29. Which of these three communication styles do you believe is most
    effective when working with men? Give examples if you can.

30. Which woman do you want to emulate in your life? Why? What can you do to improve your communication style in your family, community, or church?

31. Pen a note to one of these three women, expressing what you learned from her life. What do you plan to say to her when you meet her in eternity?

# Exchange Worry for Peace

*Mary and Martha, Friends of Jesus*

**OPTIONAL**

Memorize Philippians 4:6–7

Do not be anxious about anything, but in every situation, by prayer and petition, with thanksgiving, present your requests to God. And the peace of God, which transcends all understanding, will guard your hearts and your minds in Christ Jesus.

When I became a Christian over thirty years ago, I carried a bad habit into my new life in Christ. I worried about everything. I thought worry showed how much I cared.

> The Bureau of Standards in Washington tells us that a dense fog covering seven city blocks, 100 feet deep, is composed of something less than one glass of water. That amount of water is divided into some 60 thousand million tiny drops. Not much there! Yet when those minute particles settle down over the city or countryside, they can blot out practically all vision. A cupful of worry does just about the same thing. We forget to trust God. The tiny drops of fretfulness close around our thoughts and we are submerged without vision. (A. Purnell Bailey; quoted in Cory, *Quotable*, 446)

What freed me from my bad habit? First, a mentor explained to me that worry was not caring—it was evidence that I did not trust God, and it was sin. Her challenge caused me to rethink my assumptions, and I began to change. Second, my immersion into God's Word over several years loosed the stranglehold of worry on my life and opened the floodgates of peace, a gift that accompanies a biblical worldview. Finally, I began to serve God through my particular gift-mix. I became an activist for Jesus— I was doing something good for the kingdom, bringing a sense of purpose to my life. All these elements combined to help me leave worry behind and enjoy an unexplainable peace with God and others. In this lesson, Jesus helps us unravel the mystery of a worry-free peace-packed life—a precious gift found only in God.

 **Read Luke 10:25–27.**

The question . . . was a good question asked with a bad motive, because the lawyer hoped to trap our Lord. However, Jesus trapped the lawyer! Our Lord sent the man back to the law, not because the law saves us (Gal. 2:16, 21; 3:21), but because the law shows us that we need to be saved. There can be no real conversion without conviction, and the law is what God uses to convict sinners (Rom. 3:20).
—Warren Wiersbe
(*Be Compassionate*, 135)

1. Who challenged Jesus? What was his question? Was he sincere? What do you think was his motivation (Luke 10:25)?

- a lawyer
- what must I do to inherit eternal life?
- He was testing Jesus

2. Jesus answered the lawyer's question with another question, leading the lawyer to ultimately answer his own question (10:27). The answer is known as the Great Commandment and encompasses in a nutshell what Jesus came to teach us. Paraphrase the Great Commandment in your own words.

To love God & your neighbor as yourself — w/ all your heart, soul, strength and mind

3. The Great Commandment contains two parts. Break it down and analyze each part. What is the essence of a life that pleases God?

To love God of your whole being — and then to love others — self included —

The lawyer knew the words of the Great Commandment but he did not understand its meaning. To ensure that we understand the meaning of the Great Commandment, Luke records two passages: the parable of the good Samaritan and Jesus' visit to the home of Mary and Martha.

 Read Luke 10:28–37.

4. Jesus begins to explain the Great Commandment by telling a now
well-known parable. What happened to the unfortunate victim in the
story (10:30)? Envision the scene as if it were a contemporary film.
(*Note:* The road from Jerusalem to Jericho descends about three thou-
sand feet in seventeen miles, and robbers often hid in rocky crevices
waiting for prey.)

*It was a man who was robbed,
beaten, stripped — left half dead.*

5. Who passed by the bleeding, unconscious victim (10:31–32)? Who
stopped and helped? Specifically, what did he do (10:33–35)?

*- a priest and a Levite*

*- Samaritan, was moved by pity
He bandaged his wounds, put
him on his own animal and
brought him to an inn where
he cared for him.*

6. Jesus identifies the three men who saw the victim—a priest, a Levite, and a Samaritan. What do you think might be the significance of their different nationalities and vocations?

The first two were Jews of high status.
The Samaritan was depised by the Jews — had low status.

DIGGING DEEPER

Research the history of Jews and Samaritans. What was their relationship in the first century? What other biblical accounts show Jesus interacting with Samaritans? What do you learn?

7. What did the lawyer need to learn (10:27, 37)? How did the Samaritan illustrate this important Christian virtue?

The lawyer needed to know that all are our neighbors.
The Samaritan even Rescued his enemy!!

8. Who is your neighbor? What is love? How do you truly "love your neighbor as yourself"? Does this mean that you give to every panhandler on the street? Adopt orphans? Choose a people-helping career? How might this look in the lives of different Christians?

*Could be any of those suggestions. Need to be led by the Holy Spirit to respond to the real need for compassion for others.*

9. In your opinion, are most Christians today "good Samaritans"? Why or why not?

*Probably not —*
- *too busy*
- *too overwhelmed by all the needs*
- *caught up in own life, w/ its own needs*

10. Have you learned to love your neighbor as yourself or does this concept send you on a guilt trip? Discuss.

- hanging in w/ RISE
- helping w/ CARITAS
- sending $ to missions & other organizations
- being willing to co-lead a grief support gp.
- writing notes to folk who are suffering.

11. What would obedience to this part of the Great Commandment look like in your life? Taking into account your gift-mix, opportunities, and resources, how might you love your neighbor in the spirit of the Great Commandment?

12. *Read Romans 2:9–10.* Can you connect the concept of doing good and serving others with a sense of peace in your life? If so, try to articulate this connection. How might an active life of service to others alleviate worry in your life and promote a sense of peace?

*Anguish and distress for those who do evil — glory, honor and peace for everyone who does good ...*

 Read Luke 10:38–42.

## LOVING GOD WITH ALL YOUR HEART, SOUL, STRENGTH, AND MIND

Now Luke records an encounter that illustrates the first part of the Great Commandment. Jesus and his disciples traveled to Bethany, a few miles outside of Jerusalem. They stayed in the home of two sisters, Martha and Mary, and their brother Lazarus. Martha is probably the older sister, in charge of the home and the meal preparation for their guests.

*Worry* comes from an Old English word that means "to strangle"—how fitting, because worry strangles the life out of us.   —Sue

13. What is Mary doing during the visit (10:39)? Try to envision her physical posture, her eyes, and the expression on her face. Describe the scene.

Mary is sitting at Jesus's ft, listening to him.

Do not worry about tomorrow, for tomorrow will worry about itself. Each day has enough trouble of its own.
—Matthew 6:34

DIGGING DEEPER

Research Jewish customs related to the role of women in the first century. Do you think Mary's choice to join the men in the living room was normal at that time? Why or why not?

14. What does Proverbs 8:34–35 reveal about the person who listens and waits on God? How often during the day do you sit down? How much time do you spend each day "listening and waiting on God"? How have personal technological devices affected your relationship with God? What does "listening and waiting on God" mean anyway?

Happy is the one listing and waiting on the Lord —

15. Jesus observed that Martha was "worried and upset about many things" (Luke 10:41). Why do you think she acted this way? What did this reveal about her character?

Jesus, living as a free Jewish male, had many clashes with the religious insiders. Instead of exercising his male privilege, he overturned the assumptions about who can have access to God. Jesus made it a point to seek out women and to engage with them in spiritual conversations. He assumed that women already knew something. He assumed that even though they were illiterate and untaught, women were still capable, out of their own life experiences, of understanding the meaning of his teachings. As disciples, the women in Jesus' life weren't mere ornaments or domestic servants. Jesus expected women to be fully engaged in the pursuit of God's Wisdom.
—Lilian Calles Barger
(*Chasing Sophia*, 124)

16. How did she attempt to get some help in the kitchen (10:40b)? Can you relate?

17. How do you think her outburst affected Jesus as he was teaching? The other guests? Mary? Has your worry caused you to say or do something you later regretted?

18. Jesus answered Martha with three statements:

- First, he observed her emotional state (10:41) and then cautioned her. What did he say? Is *your* life composed of "many things"?

  *You are worried about many things*

- Second, he explained that only one thing was needed in this situation (10:42a). What do you think he meant?

  *Mary has chosen the better path – which will never be taken from her –*

- Third, Jesus credited Mary's response to his presence as praiseworthy (10:42b). Why was Mary's way better?

19. In light of Jesus' teaching on the Good Samaritan, was Jesus rebuking Martha because she was serving others? If Mary had been habitually lazy or self-absorbed, do you think Christ would have praised her (2 Thessalonians 3:6–10)? What do you think Christ was *really* teaching us in 10:38–42?

  *Taking advantage of an opportunity to learn more about Christ and lets he in takes precedent.*

Worry affects the circulation, the heart, the glands, the whole nervous system, and profoundly affects the health.
—purportedly, Dr. Charles Mayo

Do not worry about your life, what you will eat or drink; or about your body, what you will wear. Is not life more than food, and the body more than clothes? Look at the birds of the air; they do not sow or reap or store away in barns, and yet your heavenly Father feeds them. Are you not much more valuable than they? Can any one of you by worrying add a single hour to your life?
—Jesus (Matthew 6:25–27)

It is not a question of contrasting the activist life to the contemplative life. It's a matter of priorities. We put listening to and learning the Word of God before service. That equips and inspires us for our service for God to others.
—Alice Mathews
(*Woman God Can Lead*, 239)

**Endless Distractions** (*3:53 minutes*). What are you doing that doesn't need to be done?

## THE CORRELATION BETWEEN WORRY, PEACE, AND SERVICE

Peace is that calm of mind that is not ruffled by adversity, overclouded by a remorseful conscience, or disturbed by fear.
—Charles Swindoll (*Tale*, 431)

20. Have you learned to "sit at Jesus' feet"? If so, how does this look in your life? If not, how can you move closer to this posture as a lifestyle? Why is this necessary for a worry-free, peace-packed life?

The Lord didn't burden us with work. He blessed us with it.
—Author unknown
(McKenzie, *14,000 Quips*, 565)

21. Have you found a way to actively serve others in a way that fits your gift-mix and personality? If so, how did you find your place of service? What does it mean in your life? How do you feel when you are involved in meaningful good works?

22. Reread the Great Commandment in Luke 10:27. What is the relationship between the two parts? Why do you think loving God precedes loving our neighbors?

23. *Read Colossians 3:15–17.* What do these verses say about peace, sitting at Jesus' feet, and doing good through service? If we combine these elements in our lives, setting sound priorities, how will that impact whether or not we fret and worry?

As a Christ follower, it's easy to mistake intention for action and stirrings for solutions. I sometimes give myself credit for being a pretty remarkable human being just because I feel angry about injustice, pain over suffering, or empathy in the face of hurt. But even the strength of my intentions is not an accurate indicator of whether or not I will take the time to act, to put my faith to work, to be the difference that Christ has empowered me to be. Defining moments are only as good as the lifestyles they translate into.

—Nancy Ortberg
(*Looking for God*, 106-7)

24. Pen a note to Mary or Martha, expressing what you learned from her life. What do you plan to say to her when you meet her in eternity?

# Shape Overload into Simplicity

## *The Weighed-Down Woman*

Have you seen the popular women's magazine *Real Simple* (www.real simple.com)? It's one of the most successful magazines in recent years. Its pages instruct women to keep it simple—in the way they decorate, cook, and live. It strikes a chord with many women because the world around us is not simple. Due to technology and accelerating change, the world is becoming more and more complex. We are linked in a mesh of connections causing information overload. The new commodity is not money but time. We never have enough time because many of us have filled our lives with so much activity and clutter. But the more connected we become, the fewer real connections many of us enjoy. In the midst of all the change, rush, noise, and confusion, we are on overload and we long for simplicity. If you feel burdened by the pace and stuff of life, this lesson is for you.

 Read Luke 13:10–17.

## A SPECIAL SUNDAY

1. Jesus was teaching in the Jewish synagogue when a woman in the crowd caught his eye. Describe her (Luke 13:11, 16).

   *She was bent over — had been for 18 yrs.!*

---

OPTIONAL

**Memorize 1 Timothy 6:6–8**
Godliness with contentment is great gain. For we brought nothing into the world, and we can take nothing out of it. But if we have food and clothing, we will be content with that.

Lord, I'm drowning in a sea of perplexity. Waves of confusion crash over me. I'm too weak to shout for help. Either quiet the waves or lift me above them. It's too late to learn to swim.
—Ruth Harms Calkin,
*Tell Me Again Lord, I Forget*
(Swindoll, *Tale*, 484)

When a person is *beaten* inside, he or she is *bent* outside. There must be a will to live. Every doctor knows this. The best of us become "bound." We need to be "loosed."
—C. M. Ward (*Sermons*, 65)

I'm in awe of this woman. If I had a crippling ailment that caused me to be bent over for eighteen years and I had called out to God without relief, I wonder if I would be faithful to worship God week after week, year after year. Yet here she is in the synagogue. What a woman of courage!   —Sue

2. Have you ever known anyone with a similar condition? If so, how did this ailment affect the person's life?

*Only one – a man –*

3. Walk around the room completely bent over to experience her normal view. If you had lived this way for eighteen years, how do you think your life would be different than it is today?

*Would not be driving!*

4. What did Jesus say and do when he saw her (13:12–13)? Envision the synagogue packed with worshippers. What did his words and actions express to those attending the service?

*That healing someone takes precidence over everything – esp. "rules".*

5. How did the crowd react (13:17)? What did the touch of the Master's hand mean for her life from that moment on?

*She was healed. She rejoiced and the crowd joined her in praising him.*

6. Can you relate physically, emotionally, or spiritually to this woman? When have you felt "weighed down" by life? What causes you to feel this way? List the stuff in life that tends to get you down.

7. Can you recall a time when Jesus lifted a burden for you? If so, please share with the group, as you are comfortable.

8. What is the heaviest burden you bear right now?

9. In verse 12, Jesus said, "Woman, you are set free from your infirmity." Do you believe that Jesus can set you free, too? If not, what hinders your belief?

10. What did Jesus say to us in Matthew 11:28–30? Even if Jesus does not respond to our prayers exactly the way we request, what does he still promise us? Why do you think his answers to our prayers are sometimes "yes," sometimes "no," and sometimes "wait"?

*"Come to me, all that are weary and carrying heavy burdens and I will give you rest ..."*

*Prayers will be answered.*

## A DIFFERENT RESPONSE

11. The crowd was delighted when Jesus released the weighed-down woman from her burden. However, the synagogue ruler expressed a different reaction. How did he feel about what had happened (Luke 13:14a)? Any ideas why he reacted so differently?

*He was indignant that Jesus would see himself above the law.*

This is the last recorded instance of Jesus teaching in a synagogue. His enemies had become so vicious, it was no longer wise or safe. But the time for his sacrifice had not yet come.

12. Instead of addressing Jesus, the Jewish ruler addressed his congregation. What did he tell them (13:14)? How many healings do you think he had performed?

*Only come on the days that are not the Sabbath to be healed. Doesn't he'd healed anyone.*

Rabbis were extremely concerned that animals be treated well, even on the Sabbath, so they created rules that would protect them. For example, on the Sabbath, you could lead an animal by a chain or rope as long as you did not carry anything (*Shabbath 5:1*). You could draw water for your animal and pour it into a trough as long as you did not hold a bucket for the animal to drink from (*Erubin 20b, 21a*).
—Leon Morris (*Luke*, 245)

13. Jesus rebuked the synagogue ruler in verses 15 and 16. Why? Did the leader value people or animals more? In a nutshell, what did Jesus say to him? What is Jesus revealing about this man?

*That he cares more about his animals than needy people.*

The religious leaders had developed a religious system with 613 laws. They chose the number 613 because that was how many separate letters were in the text containing the Ten Commandments. Then they found 613 commandments in the Pentateuch (the first five books of the Old Testament). They divided the list into affirmative commands (do this) and negative commands (don't do this). There were 248 affirmative commands, one for every part of the human body, as they understood it. There were 365 negative commands, one for each day of the year. They further divided the list into binding commands and nonbinding commands. Then they spent their days debating whether the divisions were accurate and ranking the commands within each division (MacArthur, *Matthew 16–23*, 337–38).

14. In what sense was the synagogue ruler "crippled" and "bent over"? In what sense is anyone burdened who refuses to turn to Christ in faith?

15. *Read Luke 11:46.* Right before Jesus taught in the synagogue, he verbally flayed the Jewish leaders at a dinner party. How did the crippled woman illustrate Jesus' rebuke?

Because the leaders by burdening the people.

DIGGING DEEPER

Study Jesus' entire interaction with the Jewish leaders that night, also known as "The Six Woes" (Luke 11:37–54). Why was Jesus so angry?

 **The Wailing Wall** (*5:30 minutes*). As Sue describes her experience at the Wailing Wall, she invites you to thank God that you are not shackled by legalism.

16. Satan was responsible for the crippled woman's physical disease, but the Jewish leaders also burdened her with their legalism, demanding that she keep all their laws. How do people today allow others to weigh them down with man-made laws and expectations? Give specific examples. (No names, please.)

Dress expectations
Club "
School "
Neighborhood "
Car "
Grandchildren "
Holiday "

17. Do you know any people who have allowed others to weigh them down with unnecessary burdens, rules, and traditions? If so, how have their lives been impacted? (No names, please.)

18. Do you allow others to burden you with man–made laws and expectations? If so, what can you do to be free?

DIGGING DEEPER

Wring out 1 Corinthians 8 to learn how to respond lovingly to people caught up in legalism, without allowing them to bind the whole congregation with their chains.

*eating vs. not eating certain food is legalism.*

## SIMPLE MODELS AND METHODS

19. Jesus was God in the flesh. He orchestrated the circumstances of his life on earth and could have been born and lived anywhere at any time he chose. Where did he decide to be born, live, and minister? What does this tell you about what God values (see, for example, Luke 2:4–7 and Matthew 8:20)?

*Prophecy was being fulfilled — house of David, born in Bethlehem God's son was born in poverty!*

20. People-pleasing also adds to many women's burdens. *Read 1 Thessalonians 2:1–6.* What was Paul's view of people-pleasing?

Paul has been mistreated, but cares not what others think a do - just wants to please God.

The cure for people-pleasing is simple. Perform for an audience of One. —Sue

21. Are you a people-pleaser? If so, who do you allow to set your priorities and calendar? Why do you allow others this power over you?

22. Would your life be simpler if you gained victory over your people-pleasing? If so, write down the changes you envision, and draft a plan. If not, how have you avoided being a people-pleaser? Or, if you are an overcomer, share helpful ideas with the group.

We'll miss contentment if keeping rather than releasing becomes our objective. We too often love things and use people, when we should be using things and loving people. We are most content when we're grateful for what we own, satisfied with what we make, and generous to those in need.

—Author unknown
(Swindoll, *Tale*, 119)

23. In contrast to the Jewish leaders, how did Paul live among the people (1 Thessalonians 2:7–9)? Why? How did his attitude and actions lighten their burdens rather than increase them?

_— like a nurse caring for her own children_

24. What did Paul teach about simplicity and the problems that love of money and stuff can cause (1 Timothy 6:6–10)?

*The root of all evil is the love of th.*

25. Neither Jesus nor Paul allowed others to weigh them down with unnecessary rules or expectations. Do you know anyone who models this strength in their lives? Why do you think they are able to live this way?

*Charlie!*

26. Summarize what you have learned about the overall lifestyles of Jesus and Paul that might help you to simplify your life.

*To stop buying stuff! clearing out what is not used — and giving it away.*

27. Do you really *want* to live a simpler life? If not, what hinders you?

28. What can you do to follow the examples of Jesus and Paul? What is one thing you can eliminate from your life that is weighing you down right now? How can you simplify your lifestyle? Be specific.

29. Write a note to the woman whose burden was lifted in Luke 13:10–17, expressing what you learned from her life. What do you plan to say to her when you meet her in eternity?

# Overcome Injustice with Prayer

## *The Tale of the Relentless Widow*

H ow many times have you heard—or said—*Why, God?*

Dear God, Charles, my cat, got run over. And if you made it happen you have to tell me why.
—Harvey (quoted in Swindoll, *Tale*, 308)

Harvey is angry over the unexplained death of his cat and he wants answers from God. Life is full of experiences that seem unfair, and our natural response, like Harvey's, is to lash out at God and demand an explanation and often a different conclusion. Shortly before Jesus went to the cross, he told his disciples a parable to prepare them for the bloody ordeal ahead. Jesus' instruction continued to help them in the years ahead as they established Christianity in a hostile world—and it helps us as we face injustice today. Ask the Lord to prepare your heart for the lesson he has designed just for you this week.

 Read Luke 18:1–8.

## A GOOD LESSON FROM A BAD EXAMPLE

1. Luke tells us the purpose of the parable before we read it. Why did Jesus share this story with his disciples and with us (Luke 18:1)?

*The parable was to prepare the disciples for what was to come.*
*The pt. is to be persistent in asking God for justice.*
*All of us have experienced unfairness!*

His parables were short stories that invited the listener to see things from a different point of view. Through parables he created a world of reversals where the first was last and the last first, where the worldly wise became fools and insiders found themselves shut out.
—Lilian Calles Barger
(*Chasing Sophia*, 38–39)

2. The judge in the story represents God the Father. Readers can easily become confused about the character of God the Father if they do not observe the text carefully and think critically. Describe the judge. What kind of man was he (18:2, 6)?

*Does not fear God or have respect for people*

**The Priority of Prayer** (*3:24 minutes*). Did you know that "God helps those who help themselves" is not in the Bible?!

3. Have you ever known a person like this judge? A dysfunctional parent? A difficult boss or coworker? A self-absorbed neighbor? How did you feel around them? (No names, please.)

4. What was the widow's ongoing request (18:3)? Is justice a subject that concerns you? Why or why not?

*[handwritten] Yes!*

5. Can you relate to the widow's frustration? Can you recall a time when an issue took far too long to be resolved? Please share.

*[handwritten] How about the Holocaust, WWI and II, slavery, racism, immigration —*

Consider the prayers you usually hear in a Bible study, small group, or Sunday school. Often these prayers are centered on health, finances, and meeting various needs in our lives and in the lives of people we love. And that's good. But how often do we pray for vindication for those who need God's justice? How often do we pray for boldness to give God glory in our words and actions? How often do we pray that God will show his presence in our ministries, churches, families, and communities? How often do we pray that his kingdom will come soon, ushering in redemption and with it, justice? I was convicted by these passages to pray differently.  —Sue

The widow was almost a symbol of helplessness. She was in no position to bribe the judge and she had no protector to put pressure on him. She was armed with nothing but the fact that right was evidently on her side (she asked for justice not vengeance) and her own persistence. But what she had she used.
—Leon Morris (*Luke*, 287–88)

DIGGING DEEPER

Research the status of widows in first-century Israel. What do you learn that enriches your understanding of her plight?

Verse 5 is translated in many Bibles with the idea of being "worn out" by her coming. The Greek word is more picturesque, meaning "to give a black eye"—figuratively, of course.

6. Why did the unjust judge ultimately give in and grant her request (18:4–5)?

Was worn down by her persistence.

7. Read Psalms 68:34 and 89:13. In what way is God the Father like the unjust judge?

• Ascribe power to God, whose majesty is over Israel; and whose power is in the skies.
• You have a mighty arm: strong is your hand, high your rt. hand

He has power

8. How is God the Father different from the unjust judge (Isaiah 49:13, 15)?

The Lord comforts his people, has compassion for them — like a woman nursing her child —

DIGGING DEEPER

Dissect Psalm 18 to learn more about God's incredible compassion.

9. After Jesus told the parable to his disciples, he explained to them how God the Father is different from the unjust judge and why we can trust our Father. What did he say (Luke 18:7–8a)?

*God will grant justice to those who ask — and will do it quickly!*

10. In 18:1, we learn that the purpose of the parable was to encourage believers to persevere in prayer and not give up. How does the story of the persistent widow encourage you to continue praying when you are discouraged or frustrated?

*To keep praying!*

11. In 18:8, Jesus says God the Father gives us justice "quickly." Have you ever prayed for justice and your prayer was not answered "quickly," or worse, from your perspective, not at all? What is the difference between your definition of *quickly* and God's definition (Psalm 90:4)?

*a 1000 yrs. in your sight are like yesterday when it is past — & like a watch in the night —*

> God created time for man. In fact, even the words "in the beginning" mark the tick of the first clock. The Trinity has no such bounds in the eternal state. A wait is time oriented, and, therefore, primarily man oriented. Perhaps among a host of other reasons, I think God often ordains a wait because He purely enjoys the togetherness of it.
> —Beth Moore (*Get Out*, 146)

12. Have you learned to pray with perseverance like the persistent widow, even when God's justice does not seem to come quickly? If so, why do you continue to pray? What do you know about God that encourages you to keep praying? Give examples.

13. Jesus ended his message by referring to his second coming, when he will return to earth to set up his kingdom. What is the challenge to our generation in Jesus' question in Luke 18:8?

*To hold our faith in God —*

 Read Luke 17:20–37.

## HOPE FOR ULTIMATE JUSTICE IN THE COMING KINGDOM

Before Jesus told the parable of the persistent widow, he instructed the Jews concerning his second coming and the kingdom he would found when he returned. In Luke 17:20–37 we can find insight into our future as an incentive to persevere in prayer.

14. What did the Pharisees ask Jesus in 17:20? What kind of kingdom do you think they were expecting?

    *A political one —*

15. Jesus told the Jewish leaders that the kingdom would not come visibly at that time (17:20–21). However, in what sense was "the kingdom" already there (17:21)? Why?

    *Because of Jesus and his followers —*

In Luke 17:21, the phrase translated "within you" in the 1984 NIV has been better rendered "in your midst" in the 2011 NIV.

16. Next Jesus turned to his disciples and instructed them concerning this future, literal thousand-year kingdom. Although many false messiahs would appear and claim to bring in a new age (17:22–23), people will be unable to miss the time when Christ ushers in this millennial kingdom. Why (17:24)? Try to envision this scene.

    *There will be lightening in the skies everywhere*

**DIGGING DEEPER**

For more details on that magnificent kingdom, see Revelation 21–22.

17. What must Jesus experience before he returns to reveal his glory (17:25)?

    *Suffering — Rejection*

18. Now Jesus explained how people would act and think prior to his ushering in this millennial kingdom. What were people doing just before judgment fell in the days of Noah and of Lot (17:26–28)? Why?

*Living their ordinary lives — trying to make ends meet, being/feeling secure.*

DIGGING DEEPER

How were men and women acting just before the great flood? How did God respond (Genesis 6:5–7)? What can we expect in the future (2 Peter 3:3–7)?

DIGGING DEEPER

What happened in the days of Lot (Genesis 19)? How do those times compare to today?

19. Describe the judgment that fell on these people (Luke 17:28–29).

*Rained fire and sulfur — destroyed all.*

The disciples wanted to know more about the Kingdom, so in Luke 17:37 they asked, "Where, Lord?" And Jesus answered indirectly with the strange words, "Where there is a dead body, there the vultures will gather." Jesus would not give them exact details of when or where, but by this statement, he may have been conveying the surety of the event. Just as we can count on vultures gathering where you find a dead body, so we can count on the kingdom coming in God's perfect place and timing.

When Christ returns in glory to usher in the millennial kingdom, those who have rejected him will reap judgment just like the people in the days of Noah and of Lot (Luke 17:30, 32). This section does not refer to the Rapture. This passage will take place at the end of the Tribulation. Those who reject him will be taken into judgment, but those who have placed their faith in him during the Tribulation will enter into millennial kingdom blessing (17:31–35).

20. How do you feel when you read prophecy concerning the future? Share your struggles and/or insight on this subject.

21. Are you ready to leave this world behind? What do you need to do to prepare yourself for the kingdom of God?

## SYNTHESIZING JUSTICE, PRAYER, AND THE FUTURE

22. In light of what you have learned in Luke 17:20–18:8, what is the relationship between justice, prayer, perseverance, and God's future kingdom? Why do you think Luke placed these passages side by side?

*The Kingdom is here now, but not fully so — and we not only need to pray for justice, we are to do it — w/ God's help.*

23. Read James 5:7–11 and relate those instructions to this lesson.

*Be patient - slow endurance - like the prophets prophets, like Job.*

DIGGING DEEPER

Research James 5:7–11, particularly the comments concerning the prophets and Job. How were they excellent examples of persistent men of prayer in the face of injustice?

24. Are you persistent in your prayers—especially in your prayers for justice and for Jesus to return?

If after my removal anyone should think it worth his while to write my life [story], . . . if he gives me credit for being a plodder, he will describe me justly. Anything beyond that will be too much. I can plod. I can persevere in any definite pursuit. To this I owe everything.
  —William Carey, the father of modern missions, in a letter to his nephew

25. Are you patient as you pray? How has this lesson made an impact on your thinking about waiting on God?

26. Do you need justice right now? In what ways have you been treated unfairly? Try to envision a place where there is justice. What do you see?

27. Pen a note to the persistent widow, expressing what you learned from her life. What do you plan to say to her when you meet her in eternity?

    *I love strong women who are not owned by power of others, esp. men. I would congratulate this widow — give her a "high five"!*

# Turn Grasping into Generosity

## *The Widow in the Temple*

A typical mother, seeing there are only four pieces of pie for five people, promptly announces she never did care for pie" (McKenzie, *14,000 Quips*, 200). I love my family dearly but I also enjoy pie. I suppose in that respect I have never been the typical mother. My upbringing did not help. My father was a military officer who taught me to be independent and self-sufficient. *God helps those who help themselves* was the motto in our home. I was taught to take care of myself, to look out for number one, and to save everything I could for my own retirement, since no one else would take care of me.

As an adult convert to Christianity, I learned about the virtue of generosity, but I was stuck in stinginess and fear. As I grew in my faith, I finally opened my clenched fist and let go. What freedom!

Jesus desires this joy for all his children and often taught about generosity in his three-year ministry on earth. Luke recorded several accounts to help us rout out our stinginess. First, let's look at the story of the quintessential woman who does not like pie. I'm working on not liking it either. Will you join me?

 Read Luke 20:45–21:4.

## AN AMAZING DISPLAY

About a third of Jesus' parables, and a sixth of the Gospels overall, deal with the issue of stewardship: how we use, spend, and give what we have for the glory of God and the good of others. Jesus was not like some TV preachers, only concerned with filling his own pockets, but he did talk about money a lot, because how we invest our resources reveals how much we trust God, and our time, talents, gifts, and treasure fuel God's work on the earth. —Sue

This account takes place during Jesus' final week on earth, before the crucifixion. The Jewish leaders put out a contract on his life. Jesus knew, yet he refused to back down.

1. Jesus pointed out particular actions of the Jewish leaders to his disciples and everyone else within earshot. What character qualities can you glean from these actions (Luke 20:46–47)?

*They want recognition, wear long robes, say long prayers – show off!*

A widow represented the most vulnerable in society, whom the pious were supposed to serve. So Jesus is making a serious charge. Apparently in managing a widow's affairs, the teachers of the law took a large cut for themselves. Their pretentious long prayers for others in the face of such inconsideration made matters worse.
—Darrell Bock (*NIV Application Commentary*, 525)

2. Immediately after lambasting the Jewish leaders, Jesus' eyes were drawn toward the temple. Contributions for running the temple were collected in trumpet-shaped receptacles. Thirteen of them were dispersed around the court of women (Bock, *NIV Application Commentary*, 526). As coins dropped into the containers, they rattled against the sides, alerting bystanders to the amount. Jesus saw two different kinds of people dropping gifts into the trumpet-shaped receptacles. Who were they and how were they different (21:1–2)?

*The wealthy gave from their abundance (no sacrifice?) and the poor widow gave all she had.*

3. How much did the widow put in (21:2)? How does Jesus measure her gift (21:3)? What do his words reveal about God's economy?

*2 coins - her "all" -*
*Invest in God's Kingdom...*

The value of two mites was about one 96th of a denarius, and a denarius was worth about 17 cents. So her gift was about one 96th of 17 cents! The amount of the gift is not what the Lord sees, but the heart behind it.   —Sue

4. Do you think Jesus is telling us that we should give away everything we have to live on? What is the point of the account?

*Hope not! But should be generous of what we have for the sake of God's Kingdom*

5. Why do you think Jesus points out this widow to his disciples right after he lambasted the Jewish leaders? What is he attempting to teach them and us?

*This poor widow is more to be admired - and emulated - than the scribes who were not only vain, but took advantage of the poor*

A Roman historian wrote that when Roman legions sacked the temple in A.D. 70, they found over two and a half million sterling in the vaults. Some of this treasure undoubtedly came from "devouring widow's houses" and the practice of changing money. Travelers coming to the temple could not use their own money but had to exchange it for temple money, and pay a fee, of course. These kinds of practices infuriated Jesus, and they should infuriate us too. How we make and use money speaks volumes about our hearts.  —Sue

6. We don't know the widow's story, nor do we know why she exhibited such amazing generosity. Would you have found it difficult to give so much? If so, why? What hinders you from generous giving?

*yes, if truly she then had nothing to keep food or secure shelter.*

*Wanting to make sure there's enough $ for care when I can no longer live on my own.*

 Read Luke 12:13–21.

## PREVIOUS TEACHING

Earlier, Jesus taught the crowds important lessons about generous living and giving. Rabbis normally arbitrated financial disputes, but Jesus refused (12:13–14). Instead, he used this request as an opportunity to teach the crowd a parable concerning a man who placed his security in the wrong things. This man was everything Jesus was exhorting his listeners *not* to be.

7. Briefly, what has happened to the rich man in 12:16–19?

*He built larger barns to store all that he had — was then going to enjoy life, but he soon died.*

8. Underline each time the rich man says "I," "my," or "myself" in verses 17–19. What was his plan? Where has he placed his security? Why was he a fool (12:20)?

*13, He was taking care of his future — his earthly fortune — thought that would feed his soul.*

*He died quickly — after building his barns — couldn't take his goods w/ him then!*

9. God had blessed the rich man. What had the man failed to do with his money? *He did not share it — he hoarded it.*

10. In verse 21, Jesus exhorts us to be "rich toward God." What do you think this means?

*To be generous – time, $, etc. – for things that build the heavenly kingdom.*

11. What do you think is the main point of the parable?

*Trusting that God will ultimately provide*

DIGGING DEEPER

Study 1 Timothy 6:3–19. What characterizes those who love money? What often happens to people who put their hope in riches instead of in God? What are the mandates for believers?

DIGGING DEEPER

Use a concordance to look up references to money in the book of Proverbs. Research and comment on principles that Solomon teaches concerning generosity.

12. Are you rich toward God? Is Jesus teaching that working hard and planning to meet the physical needs of ourselves and our families are wrong? When can it become wrong?

*It's not wrong to be good stewards of what we have – It's only wrong when having "things" prevents generosity to others.*

 Read Luke 12:22–34.

## A HUGE HINDRANCE

13. What can we learn by "considering" the ravens and the lilies (Luke 12:22–24, 27–30)? What question does Jesus ask in 12:25? How would you answer?

*God takes care of the ravens and the lilies - will certainly take care of us. Worrying is useless - does not add an hr. to life.*

14. List the key concepts in verses 31–34.

- *Strive for God's kingdom - the rest will be cared for -*
- *Do not be afraid - trust*
- *Sell possessions, give alms*
- *Where your treasure is, there is where your heart is also -*

15. Do you worry often? What about? How does worry hinder generosity?

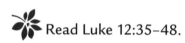 Read Luke 12:35–48.

## THE PARABLE OF THE WISE MANAGER

One of the greatest cures for fear and worry is to contemplate Christ's second coming and all the future blessings ahead for believers in God's kingdom. Christ exhorts his disciples, "You also must be ready, because the Son of Man will come at an hour when you do not expect him" (Luke 12:40).

People in Jesus' day were not ruled by their wristwatches—they did not own any. Thus, the community knew generally when a wedding feast would occur, but never exactly. A servant would make the rounds, calling guests to the festivities. And guests never knew exactly when the feast would end. Some went on for several days. Consider the Middle Eastern economy of time as you study this parable. —Sue

16. After counseling his disciples not to worry, Jesus exhorts them to be like wise and faithful managers as they await his return (12:35–48). What can a master expect from a good servant (12:35–38, 42–43)?

One who stays alert, prepared for his return

17. What tempts a servant when the master is away for a long time (12:45)? Is it easier to be a good servant when you see the master every day? What is the practical lesson for us?

*handwritten: • Beating other slaves, eating, drinking, getting drunk.*

*handwritten: To never neglect spiritual disciplines – to be living a life that is pleasing to God.*

18. What happens to the disobedient, unfaithful servant (12:46)? The ignorant servant (12:48a)?

*handwritten: • Cut to pieces / Part of the unfaithful*

*handwritten: • Will get a light beating*

Luke 12:46 includes harsh words that reveal the seriousness of living irresponsibly when serving the Lord. However, the last word in the verse is better translated *unfaithful* rather than *unbelievers.* —Sue

**DIGGING DEEPER**

When Jesus says the lazy servant will be "cut to pieces," "assigned a place with the unbelievers" and "beaten with blows," is he saying that those who are disobedient will lose their salvation? Research correct interpretive principles for parables, as well as how to determine what Jesus meant in Luke 12:46–47.

19. What will the faithful servant gain (12:44)? What do you think Jesus means?

*handwritten: Will be put in charge of all possessions.*

20. Reread verse 48b. In what sense have you been given much? Little? How are these verses an expression of the just character of God?

Have been given much.

21. Are you a good manager of the abilities, gifts, and resources God has given you? Are you comfortable with your limitations?

22. What does the parable of the wise manager teach us about generous living and giving?

It shows what we care about

 Read Matthew 20:1–16.

## A PARABLE ABOUT EQUITY

23. Jesus sets up the story in Matthew 20:1–2. What happens?

*The Kingdom of God is like a landowner hiring men to help harvest his vineyard*

24. At the third hour (9 AM), the sixth hour (12 noon), the ninth hour (3 PM), and the eleventh hour (5 PM), what did the landowner do (20:3–7)?

*He keeps hiring men —*

25. What happened when the foreman paid each worker his wages (20:8–12)? Can you relate to the frustration of the workers who began at 9 AM? Why do you feel this way?

*All got the same pay — seemed unfair*

26. How did the landowner answer the disgruntled workers (20:13–16)?

I choose to give to this last the same as I did to the others. Take what belongs to you!
I am being generous — "The last will be first, and the first will be last."

27. What do you think Jesus was attempting to teach the Jewish leaders? The disciples? Believers today?

The advantages of being called to serve the Kingdom of Israel are the same for all — no matter when one enters.

28. Do you hold tight to your resources because of the possibility of unfairness? In your opinion, what is the relationship between equity and generosity?

Helping to establish equity can be costly.

29. Giving of ourselves and our resources takes great faith, especially in "down times." What kinds of thinking squelch generosity?

- Being tired, discouraged
- Not certain it will be spent well —

Have you ever stopped to think that Christ never gave anyone money? The riches of the world were His for the taking, and His to give away, yet when the poor and hungry came to Him, He didn't give them money, and He rarely gave them food; He gave them love and service and the greatest gift of all—Himself.
—Author unknown
(Cory, *Quotable*, 155)

30. What were you taught as a child about generosity? Has this training helped or hindered you when you face a decision related to giving?

It should go to Nineveh —
Being generous will be rewarded

 **Generous Giving** (*3:02 minutes*). Are you able to trust God's provision and place your hands in his?

31. What fears hinder you from living with a generous heart?

32. How can you overcome your fears and find the freedom that accompanies generosity? What actions can you take right now to show you are generous and unafraid?

33. Pen a note to the widow who gave so much in the temple, expressing what you learned from her life. What do you plan to ask her when you meet her in eternity?

# Works Cited

Allender, Dan. *The Wounded Heart*. Colorado Springs: NavPress, 1992.

Arndt, William. *Bible Commentary: The Gospel According to St. Luke*. St. Louis, MO: Concordia, 1956.

Barclay, William. *The New Daily Study Bible: The Gospel of Luke*. Louisville, KY: Westminster John Knox, 2001.

Barger, Lilian Calles. *Chasing Sophia: Reclaiming the Lost Wisdom of Jesus*. San Francisco, CA: Josey-Bass, 2007.

Bock, Darrell. *NIV Application Commentary*. Grand Rapids: Zondervan, 1996.

Cory, Lloyd. *Quotable Quotations*. Wheaton, IL: Victor Books, 1985.

Edwards, Sue, Kelley Mathews, and Henry Rogers. *Mixed Ministry: Working Together as Brothers and Sisters in an Oversexed Society*. Grand Rapids: Kregel, 2008.

Haggai, John Edmund. *How to Win Over Worry: Positive Steps to Anxiety-Free Living*. Updated edition. Eugene, OR: Harvest House, 2009.

Hubbard, Elbert. *The American Bible*. Elbert Hubbard's Selected Writings Part 12. Whitefish, MT: Kessinger, 1942.

Hudson, Jackie. "People Grow Better in Grace." *Worldwide Challenge* magazine. April 1988.

James, Carolyn Custis. *When Life and Beliefs Collide*. Grand Rapids: Zondervan, 2001.

Kraft, Vickie. *Facing Your Feelings*. Dallas, TX: Word, 1996.

Lewis, C. S. *Mere Christianity*. New York: Macmillan, 1967.

Lucado, Max. *God Came Near: Chronicles of the Christ*. Nashville: Thomas Nelson, 1987. All rights reserved.

MacArthur, John. *Matthew 16–23*. Vol. 3. MacArthur New Testament Commentary series. Chicago: Moody Press, 1988.

Mathews, Alice. *A Woman God Can Lead*. Grand Rapids: Discovery House, 1998.

McKenzie, E. C., comp. *14,000 Quips & Quotes: For Speakers, Writers, Editors, Preachers, and Teachers*. Grand Rapids: Baker, 1990.

Moore, Beth. *Get Out of That Pit: Straight Talk About God's Deliverance*. Nashville: Integrity, 2007.

Morgan, G. Campbell, *The Gospel According to Luke*. Old Tappen, NJ: Fleming H. Revell, 1931.

Morris, Leon. *Luke*. Tyndale New Testament Commentary series. Grand Rapids: Eerdmans, 1988.

Niequist, Shauna. *Bittersweet: Thoughts on Change, Grace, and Learning the Hard Way*. Grand Rapids: Zondervan, 2010.

Ortberg, Nancy. *Looking for God*. Carol Stream, IL: Tyndale, 2008.

Ortland, Ray. *Intersections: Crossroads in Luke's Gospel*. Waco, TX: Word, 1988.

Priolo, Lou. *Pleasing People: How Not to Be an "Approval Junkie."* Phillipsburg, NJ: P&R Publishing, 2007.

Rice, John R., compiler. *Poems That Preach*. Murfreesboro, NT: Sword of the Lord, 1952.

Spiegelberg, Nancy, and Dorothy Purdy. *Fanfare: A Celebration of Belief*. Portland, OR: Multnomah, 1981. Used by permission. Poem available at http://www.godthoughts.com/fanfr.html.

Stanley, Charles. *The Gift of Forgiveness*. Nashville: Thomas Nelson, 1987, 1991.

Sullivan, Barbara. *The Control Trap*. Minneapolis, MN: Bethany House, 1991.

Swindoll, Charles R. *Growing Strong in the Seasons of Life*. Portland, OR: Multnomah, 1983.

Swindoll, Charles R. *Tale of the Tardy Oxcart and 1,501 Other Stories*. Nashville: Thomas Nelson, 1998.

ten Boom, Corrie, with Jamie Buckingham. *Tramp for the Lord*. New York: Jove Books, 1978.

Vamosh, Miriam Feinberg. *Women at the Time of the Bible*. Israel: Palphot, 2007.

Walvoord, John, and Roy Zuck. *The Bible Knowledge Commentary: New Testament*. Wheaton, IL: Victor Books, 1983.

Ward, C. M. *Sermons from Luke*. Tulsa, OK: Harrison House, 1982.

Wiersbe, Warren. *Be Compassionate*. Second edition. Colorado Springs: David C. Cook, 2010.

Winner, Lauren F. *Girl Meets God: A Memoir*. New York: Random House, 2007.

Yarmolinsky, Jane Vonnegut. *Angels Without Wings*. Boston: Houghton Mifflin, 1987.

# About the Author

Sue Edwards is associate professor of Christian education (her specialization is women's studies) at Dallas Theological Seminary, where she has the opportunity to equip men and women for future ministry. She brings over thirty years of experience into the classroom as a Bible teacher, curriculum writer, and overseer of several megachurch women's ministries. As minister to women at Irving Bible Church and director of women's ministry at Prestonwood Baptist Church in Dallas, she has worked with women from all walks of life, ages, and stages. Her passion is to see modern and postmodern women connect, learn from one another, and bond around God's Word. Her Bible studies have ushered thousands of women all over the country and overseas into deeper Scripture study and community experiences.

With Kelley Mathews, Sue has coauthored *New Doors in Ministry to Women: A Fresh Model for Transforming Your Church, Campus, or Mission Field*; *Women's Retreats: A Creative Planning Guide*; and *Leading Women Who Wound: Strategies for an Effective Ministry*. Sue and Kelley joined with Henry Rogers to coauthor *Mixed Ministry: Working Together as Brothers and Sisters in an Oversexed Society*.

Sue has a doctor of ministry degree from Gordon-Conwell Theological Seminary in Boston and a master's in Bible from Dallas Theological Seminary. With Dr. Joye Baker, she oversees the Dallas Theological Seminary doctor of ministry degree in Christian education with a women-in-ministry emphasis.

Sue has been married to David for forty years. They have two married daughters, Heather and Rachel, and five grandchildren. David is a CAD applications engineer, a lay prison chaplain, and founder of their church's prison ministry.

Mother's mother.
Deborah's parents - Jim and Kay
Mary

Debbie - young mother (Mary Ann's concern)
Martha - plan retirement - will be 75 soon.
   neighbors to know Jesus
Dorothy - wanting to see purpose in her cancer journey -
   needs better days more often
   christmas holiday, son
Peggy - Kelsey sister's generosity - amazing!
Mary B - another speck etc.? clue (here in R.)
   safe travels for Meredith / wedding
Melissa - Motherhood
Margaret - gratitude / peace -
Barbara - joy - girls and grandchildren
   harmony!
Mary - family during the holiday
   Marshall - depression